Massachusetts
on the Sea

1630 ★ 1930

Published by

THE COMMONWEALTH OF MASSACHUSETTS

In commemoration of the enterprise of the
seamen of the Massachusetts Bay Colony
and
in recognition of the maritime accomplishments of their descendants.

Compiled by

MARINE COMMITTEE

Appointed by

MASSACHUSETTS BAY COLONY
TERCENTENARY COMMISSION
MCMXXX

OTHER TITLES AVAILABLE THROUGH CONVERPAGE:

Visit www.converpagestore.com for details and pricing. Watch our library grow!

CONVERPAGE SPECIALIZES IN THE REPRODUCTION OF
RARE AND OUT-OF-PRINT BOOKS

ISBN: 0-9815720-5-7

Digitally reproduced in 2008 by:
Converpage - *Digital Reproductions*
23 Acorn Street, Scituate, MA 02066
www.converpage.com

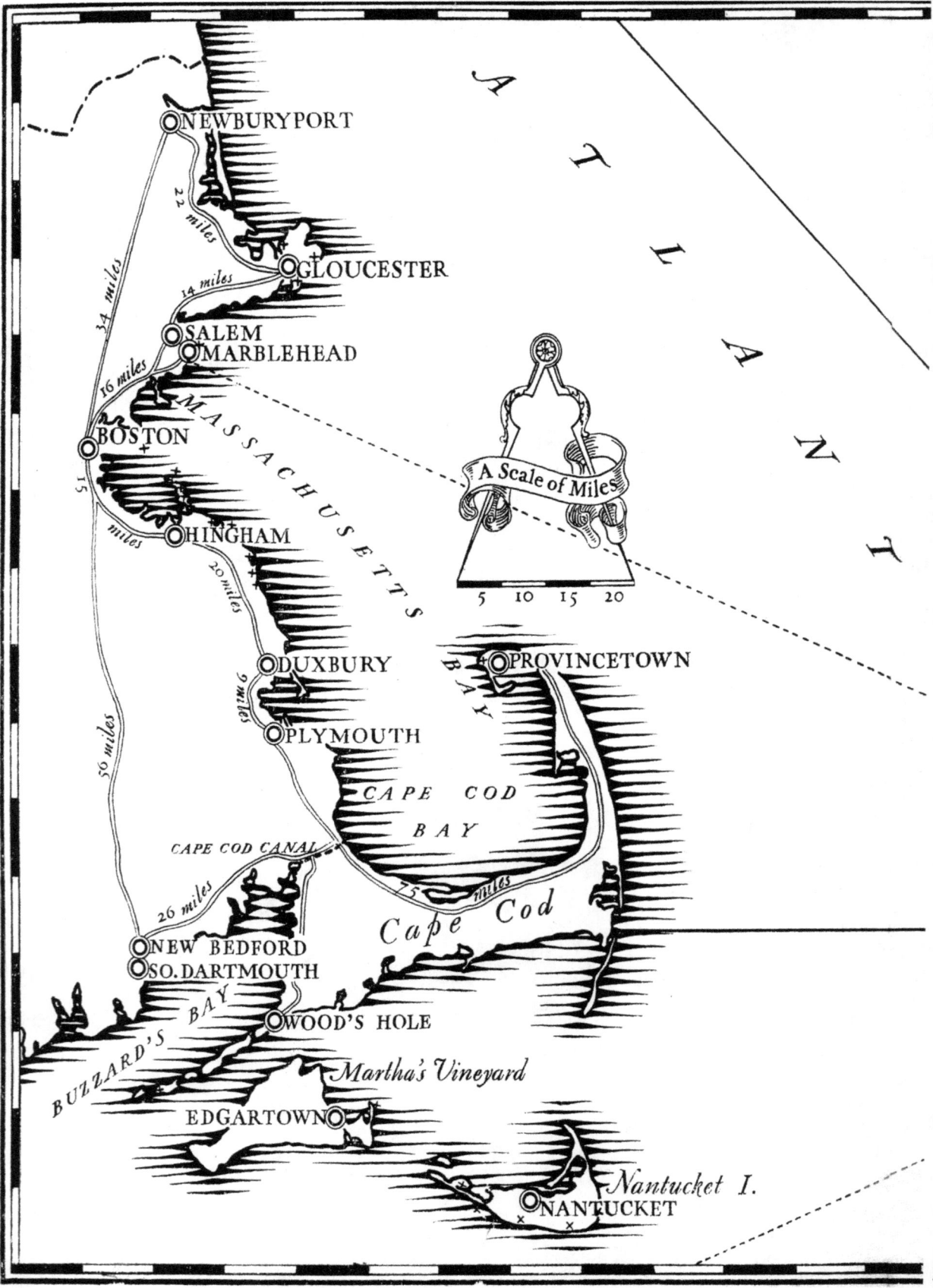

ATLANTIC

NEWBURYPORT

22 miles

34 miles

14 miles

GLOUCESTER

16 miles

SALEM
MARBLEHEAD

MASSACHUSETTS

BOSTON

15

miles

HINGHAM

20 miles

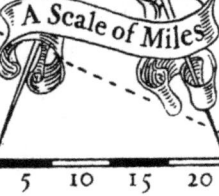

A Scale of Miles

5   10   15   20

50 miles

DUXBURY

9 miles

PLYMOUTH

PROVINCETOWN

BAY

CAPE COD

BAY

CAPE COD CANAL

75 miles

26 miles

Cape Cod

NEW BEDFORD
SO. DARTMOUTH

BUZZARD'S BAY

WOOD'S HOLE

Martha's Vineyard

EDGARTOWN

Nantucket I.
NANTUCKET

MASSACHUSETTS ON THE SEA

★ LEGEND ★

Motor Highways....

Life Saving Stations......×

N

W   E

S

A T L A N T I C

O C E A N

Courtesy of Bostonian Society.

BOSTON IN 1768

A rare engraving by Paul Revere

Tercentenary Marine Committee

Honorary Chairman

CHARLES FRANCIS ADAMS

Chairman

THORVALD S. ROSS

Vice-Chairman

CHARLES P. CURTIS

A. PIATT ANDREW	S. E. MORISON
WILLIAM L. CARLETON	HENRY A. MORSS
LAURENCE CURTIS	ROBERT E. PEABODY
ALLAN FORBES	JONATHAN S. RAYMOND

LLEWELLYN HOWLAND

Secretary

T. M. PRUDDEN

★

THESE pages have been written to welcome
the visitors to our Tercentenary Celebra-
tion and acquaint them with the maritime story
of our Commonwealth. Our colonial fishermen
and traders, our privateers of the Revolution
and 1812, our whalers and our clipper ships
wrought trade routes and founded industries,
fought battles and built fortunes not for Massachusetts alone, but for our nation. The volumes
mentioned in the bibliography, and the marine
exhibits described herein will adequately satisfy
the questions which we hope this book will
suggest.

That the spirit of our sea-loving ancestors
still lives in our young men and women may
best be judged by viewing the regattas which
take place throughout the summer off our
shores.

★

The Sea-Story of Massachusetts

By GEORGE CASPAR HOMANS AND SAMUEL ELIOT MORISON

Wide-awake Down-Easters
No-mistake Down-Easters
Old Massachusetts will win the day!

★

COLONIAL ENTERPRISE

FOR nearly three centuries Massachusetts has gone down to the sea in ships, for business and pleasure. It was not however a romantic "lure of the sea" that founded the premier maritime commonwealth of the United States, but an intense desire in Yankee people to get ahead in the world. Almost all the puritan settlers came here to be farmers. They found on the one side endless stone walls to be built around hard-scrabble upland and pastures hardly worth the clearing; on the other, inshore shoals and offshore banks where great store of codfish swam in cool green water. Not that Massachusetts has a longer coast line, or better harbors, or superior material advantages to her sister states. She was nearer the fishing banks than most of the other early settlements, but had no better supply of timber and always lacked a great staple, like cotton, for an export cargo. It was, however, enterprise, the energy of the Puritans and the sagacity of their successors which made the name of Massachusetts famous wherever ships penetrate. It is no accident that the Indians of Vancouver Island still refer to all Americans as "Boston men." It is said that South Sea Island cannibals, before deciding to cook a shipwrecked mariner, used to enquire if he hailed from Salem. If so, he was rejected as too tough.

Just as the Lord Chamberlain of England sits on a woolsack in the House of Lords as a reminder to protect the ancient staple of that kingdom, so a wooden model of a codfish was early hung up in the old State House to remind the legislators to protect their ancient industry. Visit its successor, now in the Representatives' Chamber on Beacon Hill. It tells more about Declarations of Independence and Constitutions than most histories. Cod-fishing began the sea-story of Massachusetts. Before any settlements were made, European fishermen knew this coast. Captain John Smith in 1614 took a shipload of dried codfish, cured on the island of Monhegan, to Spain—New England's first export. Fishing was one of the great inducements for settling the country and to-day is the one maritime industry in which Massachusetts still leads.

Although open boats were built by the earliest settlers, for fishing and coasting, and some of them may have made long voyages, the authentic beginning of the New England ship-building industry was the launching of Governor Winthrop's *Blessing of the Bay* on the Mystic River, from his Ten Hills Farm, on July 4, 1631. A large number of shipwrights, carpenters and artisans had been induced to come over with the other settlers in the first Puritan emigration. They found the New England oak, pine and hackmatack admirably suited for shipbuilding.

Yet Massachusetts did not take much to the sea until 1642, when the Civil War in England cut off the supply of immigrants. "All foreign commodities grew scarce," wrote Governor Winthrop, "and our own of no price. These straits set our people on work to provide fish, clapboards, plank and to look out to the West Indies for a trade." The favorite type of vessel for this trade was the ketch, a two-master, with square sail on the mainmast and a lateen on the mizzen. In 1713 the first schooner was built by Captain Andrew Robinson at Gloucester, where, two hundred years later, the world's finest schooners were owned. The schooner was the most important contribution of colonial Massachusetts to maritime progress. These little market-seekers, schooner or ketch, seldom over sixty feet long and sailed by four or five men and boys, took cargoes of fish, provisions and lumber as far as the Barbados and returned with cocoa, sugar, and molasses from the islands, dyewood from the Spanish main, and clinking pieces of eight. Some of them lost all they had to pirates, others made so much money that they were suspected of piracy themselves, and if caught, hanged on Bird Island or Nix's Mate in Boston Harbor (It was the mate of Captain Nix who in his dying speech protested his innocence, and foretold that the island, where once sheep were pastured, would sink to prove it. And so it has!). Vessels a little larger handled the tobacco crop of Maryland and Virginia, and North Carolina, and made voyages to England.

It is hard for us to realize now the importance of the West India sugar islands in the eighteenth century. A single island like Martinique was

Cap Cook Cast a Way on Cape Cod 1802

considered as valuable as the whole of Canada, so when Edward Randolph as early as 1676 called Boston the "mart town of the West Indies," he said a great deal. According to his report four hundred and thirty vessels, some as large as two hundred and fifty tons, were built and owned in Massachusetts. Massachusetts was supplying provisions to the islands and, in turn, was handling their products. Outside of the West Indies the trade was largely confined to the southern colonies and England, although occasionally larger vessels would visit the coast of Africa or even round the Cape of Good Hope to trade with the pirates at Madagascar.

What of the slave trade? Massachusetts has always been accused of laying the seeds of the evil which Yankee reformers were the first to attack. West India molasses was made into rum at Boston, Salem and Medford. Rum bought negroes on the Guinea coast. Then came the horrible middle passage of this triangular trade, and finally the slaves were disposed of in the West Indies and the southern colonies. Certainly this was done, in the seventeenth and eighteenth centuries, when even royal princes and great merchants were not averse to taking profits from the trade in negroes.

> O! Captain Ball was a Yankee slaver,
>   Blow, boys, blow
> He traded in niggers and loved his Savior,
>   Blow, my bully boys, blow.

But the slave trade was never a leading interest in Massachusetts.

It was largely interference with her legitimate West India trade, so vital to her existence, that made sea-board Massachusetts so forward in the patriotic cause. The colonies valued liberty, but their first need was to live, and the new regulations passed by the English Parliament, such as placing prohibitory duties on molasses, were irritating, if not destructive. The closing of the port of Boston in 1774 in retaliation for the Boston Tea Party, shows that Parliament knew what the New England prosperity was built on. The War of Independence resulted in the fishing fleet being laid up, and the whaling fleet, which the Nantucketers had built up to a point that aroused the eloquence of Edmund Burke, being entirely wiped out; but the seaports of Massachusetts, from Haverhill around to Westport, found plenty of employment as well as enjoyment in privateering. By constantly intercepting British army supplies to the benefit of Continentals, and making English trade dangerous and ineffective, the Yankee privateers had an important part in winning the war.

INDEPENDENCE AND THE FAR EAST

The peace of 1783 found most of the Massachusetts privateer owners—except the canny Cabots who had salted down their profits in Spain,—ruined by over-speculation; the fishing fleet was rotting from disuse, and what was worse, the protected market in the British Empire was closed, or become competitive; and the French West Indies were none too favorable. The period is marked by hard times, and by disturbances like Shays' rebellion; but the Yankees pulled their belts in a hole or two, rerigged their privateers as merchantmen, caulked the old-timers and spread their sails for new markets.

In December 1783, the fifty-five ton sloop *Harriet* of Hingham sailed from Boston with a cargo of ginseng—for China, but sold out at the Cape of Good Hope to some British East-Indiamen who were afraid of Yankee competition. Though the intentions of the Bostonians had been good, the ship *Empress of China* of New York had the honor to fly the first American flag in Canton. Her supercargo, or owner's representative on board was Major Samuel Shaw of Boston. And in 1787 the ship *Grand Turk* of Salem returned from the first Massachusetts voyage to the Far East. Salem was first in the field and she followed up her advantage.

It was extremely difficult for Massachusetts to find an export cargo to pay for the silks, teas and chinaware of Canton. Chinamen cared nothing for rum, salt pork, dried codfish, or barrel staves. A lading for the East Indies had to be assembled out of several corners of the earth: Yankee notions, Madeira wine, West India goods; and sold for specie in India before Canton could be approached. Boston, however, found a short cut. In 1784 the story of Captain Cook's last voyage to the Pacific was published; an American, Lieutenant Gore, had been his third in command and had brought the ship home. The narrative told, among other things, of a few sea-otter skins from the northwest coast of the American continent which the Chinese at Canton had snapped up greedily. On August 9, 1790, the ship *Columbia* of Boston returned from China, the first American ship to sail around the world. Her Captain, Robert Gray, had peddled

SHIP "ULYSSES" OF SALEM

Here is shown an unusual ship repair at sea; shipping a temporary rudder

his cargo of trinkets along the Northwest coast in exchange for furs, which he had sold at Canton. Here was a triangular trade with a vengeance, and the proper key for unlocking the East. In 1792 on her second voyage, the *Columbia* discovered the mouth of the river which was later named after her. Boston had taken her first steps in world commerce.

Boston and Salem exceeded any other American ports in the volume of their Far Eastern trade. Salem, Marblehead, and New Bedford in those days ranked among the first ten American ports. On both sides the trade broadened out. The Bostonians found that the Hawaiian Island sandal-wood was acceptable at Canton. In 1793 a Salem schooner under Captain Jonathan Carnes, clearing for an unknown destination, brought home a cargo of pepper from Benculen in Sumatra. Coffee from Mocha, cottons from Calcutta, hemp from Manila: the profits piled up. *Divitis Indiae usque ad ultimum sinum* on the Salem city seal meant what it said: "To the furthest gulf for the wealth of India."

Equal enterprise was shown in Western waters. These were the years of the revolution in France, the Napoleonic wars, of orders in council and paper blockades, and of the iron grip of the British fleet on the coasts of Europe. Europe was divided into two armed camps with the Americans the friends of both parties. Newburyport, Plymouth, Marblehead, indeed all the Massachusetts ports, large and small, sent their schooners or their 250-ton ships, heavily armed, to carry a great part of the trade of the dis-organized continent. With an enterprising and bold master—and few of them were not—even the smallest vessels could pay for themselves and leave a huge profit over in a few voyages between European ports or from Massachusetts to the continent. The various routes were closely interlocked. In May 1784, George Cabot of Beverly opened the American trade with Russia, over half of which was later controlled by one Massa-chusetts firm. From the Baltic the ships returned with canvas, hemp, and iron, for new vessels. The Mediterranean was full of New England ships with lumber and fish, bringing back salt, fruit, and wine. East and West India products were used for the larger ventures. During the naval hostili-ties with France (1798–1800) ships such as the *Mount Vernon* of Salem received letters of marque and mounted as many as twenty guns. She beat off the attacks of a French frigate and two Algerine pirates on the way to Gibraltar in 1799. In 1807 Jefferson's embargo ended these days of bumper trade.

Massachusetts seamen were prepared to find their way to Canton with log, lead and compass. Very few of the smaller vessels in European trade carried charts, much less quadrants. Chronometers, being expensive, were discouraged. There is the story of the English sea-captain who wished to make New York from England. He was told to sail west until he ran into a fleet of men fishing in little boats. They would give him the course. These Massachusetts shipmasters, navigating in similar fashion, knew the Atlantic as they did their backyards at home, and in their little apple-cheeked ships they could afford to sail until they found bottom with the dipsey lead. An important by-product of Massachusetts shipping was Nathaniel Bowditch, born at Salem in 1773. Interested from boyhood in mathematics and astronomy, he had leisure in long voyages as supercargo, to discover the weaknesses of the contemporary navigational tables and work up correct ones of his own. His "American Practical Navigator" was published in 1801 at Newburyport and a "Bowditch" is still in the chart house of every American ship.

If you wish to catch the atmosphere of the Federalist era in Massachusetts go to Salem and visit the Peabody Museum with its ship-portraits by that prince of marine artists, Anton Roux of Marseilles. Then walk up Chestnut Street and catch the sense of proportion that architects learn in a maritime community. Think of the owner scanning the harbor entrance from the roof of his house for the ship that will make his fortune or ruin him utterly. And think of the Straits of Sunda with an East-Indiaman homeward bound, her crew at her guns for fear of Malays, the island astern, a fragrance of cloves and mangosteen, the East asleep in an evening sea.

In 1801 Jefferson defeated Adams for the Presidency of the United States, and the Federalist party, which spoke for maritime New England, went permanently out of national power. New forces from the South and West began to control the country. The Massachusetts merchants held no grudge against Great Britain. She stood for reliability. They had banking connections in London. The British fleet had been tolerant of their neutral traders and had not done nearly as much impressing of seamen as the Western fire-eaters declared. From December 1807 to March 1809 Jefferson's embargo, by holding the foreign commerce of the United States in port, impoverished the principal ship-owning commonwealth of the nation, without ever disturbing Great Britain. There was a

The Letter of Marque. Brig Grand Turk, of 14 Guns, W.ᵐ Austin Com.ʳ ↄ Saluting Marseilles, 1815

Courtesy of Peabody Museum of Salem.

A Famous Privateer of Salem

short and profitable three years of trade until 1812, and then war made the New England marine fair game again. This war for "free trade and sailor's rights" was declared by those Americans who knew neither trade nor sailors. Massachusetts took half-heartedly to privateering, the famous ship *America* of the Republican Crowninshield family of Salem being the most successful. In the last years of the war, so much New England shipping had been either captured or blockaded that the New England press began to talk of secession; but wiser counsels prevailed at the Hartford Convention of 1815.

THE ICE TRADE AND WHALING

The World peace of 1815 brought back the full competition of the European nations. The little ports were swallowed up by Boston; they did not have the backing to keep on in a day of larger ships and a greater volume of commerce. Salem drowsed slowly away, nursing her specialties— the traffic with both coasts of Africa, with Fiji, and Manila. The last Salem East Indiaman *Mindoro* left Derby Wharf in 1893. It says a great deal for the energy of the Bostonians, though they were supported by an influx of ex-Salem merchants and Cape Cod seamen, that they kept on as well as they did. The opening of the West, the Erie Canal, and the railroads, emphasized Boston's great natural disadvantage—the Berkshire barrier. The center of gravity was moving westward; New York became the natural gate to America, though Boston remained the larger ship-owning port until 1843. "Infant industries," supported by an infant tariff, had sprung up during the long separation from Europe. The smaller seaports took to cotton mills, such as the Naumkeag at Salem and the Wamsutta at New Bedford. The tariff kept East India cottons out of the country, but the new industries at last produced something for an export cargo. The real trouble was that Massachusetts ships were no longer manned by Yankees. The farmer boys, looking for opportunities, went West or to the cities, not to sea.

Boston, however, still went on to unparalleled prosperity. A large number of the old routes were still profitable. The hide trade with South America and California, immortalized in R. H. Dana's "Two Years Before the Mast," took the place of Northwest fur trade and supplied the Lynn shoe-shops. Hawaii remained a center for missionaries, Boston traders, and riotous whalemen. In the Mediterranean, the fast Boston brigs and schooners did an ever-increasing business in wines and fruits. In 1843 the American consul at Genoa wrote: "Some years, more than half the vessels entering this port have been owned by Robert Gould Shaw of Boston." Splendid docks were built, such as Central Wharf in 1819. The Boston and Liverpool Packet Company was founded in 1822, but failed in 1827 and Boston had to wait until 1844 for the Train line to give an adequate service.

A dignified and respectable commerce in tea, with occasional darker dealings in opium, continued with China in the fine 500-ton Medford-built Indiamen (stout, business-like ships with nothing flashy about them); but a more transcendent turn of Yankee ingenuity was on the way. Frederick Tudor of Boston shipped one hundred and thirty tons of Saugus pond ice to Martinique in 1805. After the war he went at it again and gradually spread his market. In 1833 the *Tuscany*, after twice passing the equator, landed the first ice cargo in Calcutta. It came just in time to preserve Boston's East India commerce from ruin. Until cheaper artificial ice was developed, the product of New England ponds was shipped to every large port in South America and the East, in spite of customers who left their purchases in the sun and demanded money back. Thoreau's Walden was "mingled with the sacred water of the Ganges," and in 1857 ninety-six out of the hundred and twelve vessels that loaded at Calcutta for the United States landed their cargoes at Boston.

"In the year 1690 some persons were on a high hill observing the whales spouting and sporting with each other, when one observed: 'there— pointing to the sea— is a green pasture where our children's grand-children will go for bread.'"—so writes Obed Macy in his "History of Nantucket." Whaling has always been the most spectacular of Massachusetts maritime enterprises. The three or four years' voyage to the outskirts of the world, the harpoon, the "Nantucket sleigh-ride," the pursuit of the primeval sea-beast Leviathan who

> "maketh a path to shine after him
> One would think the deep to be hoary,"

has always gripped the imagination: witness Melville's "Moby Dick," which has lately come into its own as the world's greatest classic of the sea. Nantucket, settled by Quaker exiles from Massachusetts and thrust

A SCHOOL OF SPERM WHALE
OFF THE ISLAND OF HAWAII

MASSACHUSETTS ON THE SEA

far out toward the Gulf Stream, was presented with whales for the catching close to shore. Exhausting this supply the Nantucketers in the eighteenth century followed their game all over the Atlantic from Greenland to Brazil. Edmund Burke in Parliament used the whaleman as the supreme example of American enterprise: "No sea but what is vexed by their fisheries."

Nantucket's fleet recovered slowly from the Revolution, but in 1791 six Nantucket whalers and one out of New Bedford entered the Pacific. After that no "secret drawer or locker of the world" from Behring Sea to the Antarctic was safe from them. Scores of Pacific islands have good Quaker names. "Two-thirds of the terraqueous globe is the Nantucketois," wrote Herman Melville. New Bedford superseded shallow-harbored Nantucket, but the industry prospered. It was a hard life for the hayseed tempted on board those little square-sterned barques by the gorgeous yarns of the shipping agents. He was ground between niggardly owners and captains, often like Ahab, half-crazy with too many years of flat seas and lonely suns, but at least he saw a great deal of the watery part of the world.

THE CLIPPER SHIP ERA

In 1849 gold was discovered in California. When a nation goes adventuring it must be fed. It was the need for ships to carry supplies round the Horn to the "diggings" with all possible speed that ushered in the clipper-ship era, but the clipper itself was not a product of the gold rush. Competition was sharp on the China run and growing sharper. Simultaneously with the story from California, came the news that Parliament had repealed the Navigation Act, thus creating a new market for Yankee-built ships in Great Britain. The honor of producing the first clipper ship went to New York in 1845, when John W. Griffith's *Rainbow* was launched. The fast Baltimore clipper brigs and schooners gave length and V-shaped cross sections; a Singapore sampan, which Captain Waterman brought home, contributed fine flaring bows. Boston was not far behind with the *Surprise* and the *Gamecock* in 1850 built by Samuel Hall and designed by Samuel H. Pook.

The Michael Angelo of the clipper ship, however, was Donald McKay. A Nova Scotian transplanted to Massachusetts, he worked his way up in his trade, and in the forties got his first important orders—for the powerful ships of Enoch Train's packet line. His first clipper was the 1500-ton *Stag-Hound* launched from his East Boston shipyard in 1850, and after her, year by year, a series of the most beautiful ships that ever took the water, becoming larger and swifter as the volume of trade continued to increase. The renowned *Flying Cloud* in 1851, then *Flying Fish, Westward Ho!, Sovereign of the Seas,* and in 1853, the huge clipper four-masted *Great Republic,* of 4555-tons burden, which was burned at her loading dock in New York and cut down drastically before she had a chance to show what was in her. Then came the 2500-ton quartet for James Baines of Liverpool and the Australian gold rush: *James Baines, Champion of the Seas, Donald McKay,* and *Lightning.*

The clipper ships usually went around the Horn from New York or Boston to San Francisco and then ran across to China to load teas. Some found their way to London and startled the "Limeys." These were the days of the fleet races, "with the great capes of the world for turning marks;" the days when two ships might leave Boston the same hour, plunge through the trades with studding-sails set, in sight of each other for days, and burst into 'Frisco on the same tide; the days of beating down the China Sea against the monsoon with the first teas of the season. Twice the *Flying Cloud* reached California in 89 days from New York; and of the clippers that could boast a day's run of over four hundred miles, all but one were designed by Donald McKay: that one, the *Red Jacket,* by Pook. These Clipper ships were our cathedrals, our classics, our old masters. If their proportion and beauty, power and sweep is overwhelming even now in pictures and models, what splendor must have been theirs when they tore out past Boston Light on their maiden passages fresh in

> "That art untouched by softness, all that line
> Drawn ringing hard to stand the test of brine,
> That nobleness and grandeur, all that beauty
> Born of a manly life and bitter duty."

Glory passes swiftly. The clippers were too expensive for all but the blue-ribbon runs. Their crews were badly paid and often inadequate to handle the huge spars and sails. Self-respecting Yankees were not often found in clipper fore-castles. Massachusetts had her fling, then came the panic of 1857 and Civil War.

Courtesy of Marine Museum, Boston.

DONALD McKAY'S "SOVEREIGN OF THE SEAS"

SINCE THE CIVIL WAR

Another war—another chapter in the sea-story of Massachusetts—the latest. The damage done the American Merchant Marine by the Confederate cruisers was great, but not irreplaceable. The real damage done by the Civil War was to fasten the industrial age on the country; to make manufacturing more profitable than shipping. The merchant who imported his goods in his own vessels and marketed them himself, was a dying caste. Pepper and rice and tea were the glamorous cargoes that made the fortunes of Salem and Boston; the new shipping era was one of bulk loadings of coal or wheat or rails; an era of rates, rail connections, and common carriers. Vessels wandered from port to port looking for freight. Wooden shipbuilding moved down the coast to Massachusetts' first-born, Maine, nearer the lumber supply. In iron and steel shipbuilding the English had a tremendous start,—and Yankee enterprise, dazzled by the success of the clippers and far from the sources of supply, showed itself unable to cope with coal, steel, and steam. The clippers themselves, most of them extremely short-lived and expensive, were discovered to be as delicate as race-horses. A more moderate type, especially Down-Easters from Bath and Searsport, and the new British iron wind-jammers, were better fitted to survive on a more prosaic ocean.

Yet if the world-wandering Massachusetts sailing ship was a doomed species, she only died by inches and enjoyed a hearty old age. Through the 'seventies Boston remained hard at the task of reaping the harvests of distant seas. After the war, the Boston house of W. F. Weld & Company, with more than fifty first-class square-riggers flying their famous Black Horse house-flag, owned the largest merchant fleet in the United States. The *Great Admiral* built at Boston in 1869, the last of the Weld ships, was not sold until 1897.

Through the changes of the centuries, the sacred but unromantic codfish remained at the bottom of New England prosperity. John Adams, in the treaty of peace with England after the Revolution, saw to it that the Grand Banks, the Gulf of St. Lawrence and the Nova Scotia coast were still open to fishermen from his native New England. The little sharp-sterned bluff-bowed "pinkies" kept close to shore, but the "heel-tappers," with their high quarter-decks, and later the more modern flush-decked square-sterned schooners brought three or four fares a season from the

Banks, "from old 'Queereau to Grand" or the tide-torn Georges. As the shore market grew, the industry kept pace, in vessels, methods, and range. Through the century the size and speed of the "Bankers" increased until, with the help of yacht-designers like Edward Burgess in the '80s and the introduction of the spoon bow a few years later, the modern "Gloucester fishermen" were developed—magnificent craft from the Essex shipyards like *Esperanto*, *Henry Ford*, and *Columbia* of Fisherman's Race fame. Trawling from dories and seining from a modified whaleboat have taken the place of hand-lining from the decks of the schooners and increased the perils of the trade. The Cape Cod and Gloucester seining fleets pursue the mackerel from the Virginia Capes to Nova Scotia from early spring to fall, while the Bankers go as far as Iceland after ground fish. In recent years, the swordfishing fleets with their pulpit bowsprits have added further variety.

Have you ever paraded home from Europe on a forty-thousand ton liner and noticed off the coast a deep four-master slatting on the swells? The coasting schooners are more American than the clipper ships and much more a Massachusetts invention. Designed on the theory that if you kept on dividing the area of sails to be handled, you could increase the size of the vessel indefinitely and still sail her with a small crew, the multi-masted coasters were the direct heirs of one of the most ancient Massachusetts trade-routes. In the 1830s the booming cotton and coal trade from the South to New England factories created the demand for big ships. Honors for the three-master went to Maine in 1831, but in 1882 the thousand-ton *Elliott B. Church* of Taunton and the larger *Governor Ames* of Boston set the style for schooners of four and five masts. By no means unseaworthy, though full-bodied, these big bulk carriers were faced with a voyage of genuine deep-sea length and difficulty, and were capable of even greater things. The *Governor Ames* thrashed round the Horn to San Francisco and returned to end her days in the trade she was designed for. Others went as far and farther. The mammoth of the lot was the 5,200-ton steel seven-master *Thomas W. Lawson*, designed by B. B. Crowninshield and launched at Fore River, Quincy, in 1902. In her the coaster theory reached its highest perfection, for with properly placed donkey engines she needed only *sixteen* men to handle her; but the story goes that it took half an hour to bring her about, and, improperly ballasted, she was lost off Scilly, Friday, December 13, 1907. The peak

A GLOUCESTER FISHERMAN

of the schooner trade had been reached two years before. As the mate of the five-master *Nancy*, stranded on Nantasket beach a few years ago, remarked: "We may take four or we may take twenty days to make Boston from Norfolk. We can't compete with the steamers."

Fishing and yachting are the two maritime activities in which Massachusetts still leads. If we except George Crowninshield's famous *Cleopatra's Barge*, Massachusetts yachting began in 1832 when Benjamin C. Clark, a Boston Mediterranean merchant, purchased the pilot schooner *Mermaid*. The retired sea-captains found in their smart little schooners some of the exhilaration of their hard-driven square riggers, and by 1845, when the first open yacht race was held at Nahant, there was a good fleet of them, but it was not until the Eastern Yacht Club was founded in 1870 that Massachusetts yachting began to mean what it does today. Marblehead has always been in the front in yacht designing from the magnificent Burgess defenders of the America's Cup in the eighties, until this year, when a Boston syndicate has built the jib-headed sloop *Yankee*, designed by Frank C. Paine, as a possible opponent to Sir Thomas Lipton's challenger. When, every August, all the fleets of Massachusetts Bay gather at Marblehead for Race Week, a larger number of yachts cross the starting line than anywhere else in the world. The building and upkeep of this fleet of pleasure boats, large and small, constitutes no mean industry. And what discipline it is for a boy to sail his own boat, to contend with elements that cannot be bluffed. What joy for a business or professional man to thrust offshore in a cruising schooner or ketch—master of his ship and of himself, as in the brave days of sail.

Massachusetts has done more than her share to officer the ships of the American merchant marine. In 1891 the General Court of the Commonwealth established the Massachusetts Nautical Training School. The United States Navy provides a training ship, first the *Enterprise*, and since 1909 the auxiliary steam barkentine, *Nantucket*, 1261 tons, a former gunboat. Here some 2500 young men of Massachusetts have been trained, during the winter in Boston and abroad on summer cruises, for watch officers and engineers in the American merchant marine. The white *Nantucket* with her masts and yards is well-known in European ports and the School has a splendid record in war and peace. At present it has six hundred graduates in the merchant service, and the demand far exceeds the supply.

In Boston harbor today the ghosts of the last days of sail are having a hard time of it; which is as it should be, for Massachusetts made her mark by being more efficient than her competitors, not more romantic. The Clyde-built steel barque *Belmont*, last of Boston's square-riggers—she had sailed in the River Plate lumber trade—left Battery Wharf in 1925 to become a barge. The last outward-bound whaling bark, *Wanderer*, had gone ashore on Cuttyhunk in a summer gale two years before, and though still later a little schooner *John S. Manta*, with the characteristic big wooden davits, was fitting out at New Bedford for a cruise for whales as far as Hatteras, she no longer sails. She was an anachronism in the days of the huge Norwegian whaling steamers. Save for an occasional "Fisherman's Race," the bankers chug out past Eastern Point or Minot's Light with heavy-duty Diesel engines, sails flaked or even unbent. The racing-fishing schooners of recent years have been unlucky, but the increasing number of steel power-trawlers is a good sign.

A few coasting schooners of the Crowell and Thurlow fleet wait in Chelsea creek for a charter, but hardly a winter passes without the news of the loss (without replacement) of one of their fine ships off the Virginia Capes or Bermuda. The World War brought back old times and many wind-jammers ran the submarine gauntlet to carry cargoes to Europe, but the final result was an oversupply of unprofitable ships. In this era, like a story from yesterday, is that of the three-masted schooner *Marion L. Conrad*, which sailed from Boston in 1929 for a trading voyage to Africa.

The gradual disappearance of the sailing ship from the high seas is however only a sign of the times to be found in almost any part of the world, and although square riggers no longer sail from Boston, the commerce of the port now far exceeds that of the clipper ship era. Boston is regularly served by lines of steamers to, and from Europe, Asia, Africa, South America, and Australia, to say nothing of the vast fleet of ships engaged in the coastwise trade. The exports through the port have declined considerably in recent years due to the creation by the Interstate Commerce Commission of the differential on rail freight from the west, but on the other hand the import trade has steadily grown. Moreover, since the opening of the Panama Canal a large traffic has sprung up between Boston and the Pacific Coast which employs many ships and greatly swells the business of the port. The coal trade from Virginia to Boston, which for

"THOMAS W. LAWSON"
5,200 tons, built at Fore River, 1902

many years was carried by the four, five and six-masted schooners, is now borne by a large fleet of efficient steam colliers, nor must one ignore the steadily increasing arrivals in the port of oil tank steamers from Texas or Mexico, a trade unthought of thirty years ago.

It is an unfortunate fact that only a small portion of the ships engaged in Boston's commerce are Boston owned, the steam collier fleet and some of the coasting lines excepted. To be sure Boston houses operate for the Shipping Board the lines of American steamers between Boston and Germany and Boston and the Argentine, but there is one Boston fleet that still is a potent factor in foreign trade.

In 1870, the schooner *Telegraph* of Wellfleet on "The Cape," Lorenzo D. Baker, master, brought home to Boston from Kingston, Jamaica, a few bunches of bananas. Bananas had been brought to the United States before, but this exploit opened the eyes of Andrew W. Preston of Beverly, a Boston banker and fruit merchant. In 1885 he persuaded nine Bostonians to advance two thousand dollars apiece to found the Boston Fruit Company for the purchase of banana land in the West Indies. In 1899 the company became the United Fruit Company. Though the ships of the world-famous Great White Fleet hail from New York, if not under foreign registry, still the United Fruit Company is one of the great Boston-founded American corporations and a lineal descendant of Governor Winthrop's West India trade. "I hold no brief for the United Fruit Company," says one writer, "but it must be said that that great corporation has done more for Central America than all other agencies combined."

One of the oldest industries of Massachusetts still continues, that of building ships. This industry, which began with the launching of the *Blessing of the Bay* in 1631, still thrives today at Quincy, on an inlet of Boston Harbor, where the Fore River Shipyards of the Bethlehem Steel Corporation are equipped to build anything from a tugboat to an ocean liner or a battleship. In 1927 this yard completed for the United States Navy the airplane carrier "*Lexington*," the biggest ship ever built in America and one of the largest vessels afloat.

The earliest settlers who came to these shores were lured here by the prospects of catching codfish, and fishing may be truly called the original Massachusetts industry. It is gratifying to know that the codfish hanging in the State House is no obsolete emblem of a forgotten era but still represents a most vital and active industry. Boston is still the premier fishing port of the country and Gloucester a close second. The South Boston Fish Pier handles ten million dollars' worth of catch a year.

Such is the maritime story of Massachusetts, three centuries old. Neutral trader and clipper ship are gone, and have left a great tradition. But beyond the tall lighthouses and the rocky coves and the estuaries that wind through sweet salt marshes, there still lies the Bay, and beyond the Bay, the sea.

* * * * * * * * * * * *

Bibliography

S. E. MORISON, *Maritime History of Massachusetts* (new Edition, 1930).

S. E. MORISON, *Builders of the Bay Colony.* 1930.
　　The chapter on John Hull tells about colonial seafaring.

ARTHUR H. CLARK, *The Clipper Ship Era.* 1910.
　　A sea classic, including a stirring account of the Massachusetts clipper ships.

ALFRED BASIL LUBBOCK, *The Down Easters.* 1929.
　　The best available account of sailing ships after 1860.

JAMES CONNOLLY, *The Book of the Gloucester Fishermen.* 1927.
　　A splendid account of the fishermen of Cape Ann, by one of them.

JOHN RANDOLPH SPEARS, *The Story of the New England Whalers.* 1908.
　　A comprehensive account of the whale fishery.

ELMO PAUL HOHMAN, *The American Whaleman.* 1928.
　　A concise and fair-minded history of New Bedford whaling.

JOHN RANDOLPH SPEARS, *The Story of the American Merchant Marine.* 1910.
　　An excellent work on the subject. Most of the others on the same topic were written to secure ship subsidies, and make wild work of the facts.

HENRY C. KITTREDGE, *Cape Cod, its People and their History.* 1930.
　　One of the best of our regional histories.

HENRY BESTON, *The Outermost House: Life on the Great Beach of Cape Cod.* 1929.
　　An impression of wild life on Cape Cod, written in a beautiful style.

WILLIAM F. MACY, *The Story of Old Nantucket* and *The Nantucket Scrap-Basket.* 1928.
　　A short history and good yarns of the island, which in itself is one of the best of our maritime exhibits.

FREDERICK UPHAM ADAMS, *The Conquest of the Tropics.* 1914.
　　A history of the United Fruit Company.

ROBERT E. PEABODY, *The Log of the Grand Turks.* 1926
　　An account of the three famous vessels of that name.

RICHARD C. McKAY, *Some Famous Sailing Ships and Their Builder, Donald McKay.* 1928.

HERMAN MELVILLE, *Moby Dick.*
　　This is the outstanding and classic story of whaling.

AIRPLANE CARRIER "LEXINGTON"

The Humane Society
of the Commonwealth of Massachusetts

THE Humane Society of the Commonwealth of Massachusetts was founded in Boston, in 1785, by a group of public-spirited citizens interested in the subject of resuscitation from apparent death. Among its earliest activities was the erecting of huts in Boston Harbor and the adjoining waters for the refuge of shipwrecked mariners. The three huts of 1787 grew to seventeen in 1806, and in the following year, the first life-boat in America was established by the Society at Cohasset. Gradually the number of life-saving stations rose to nearly one hundred in 1869, and the long record of rescues performed by the Society's Captains and crews is among the brightest pages in the history of our Commonwealth. The wreck of the *Tremont* at Hull in 1884, of the *City of Columbus* off Gay Head, forty years later, and in more recent years of the *Norseman*, off Marblehead—these, and dozens of other similar disasters, gave occasion for the display of heroism and seamanship of which Massachusetts may well be proud.

In 1879 the Society first made use of the Hunt gun and apparatus, designed to throw a lifeline to a wreck and to bring ashore passengers and crew in the breeches buoy, and this ingenious device has been the means of saving many lives.

With the establishment of the United States Life Saving Service in 1871, and the development of storm warnings, wireless, and the auxiliary power equipment of modern vessels, a shipwreck on our coast has become a rarity instead of a common occurrence. Gradually, therefore, the Humane Society has discontinued its stations until less than a score remain, and instead has undertaken a number of more modern activities—the teaching of children to swim, the safeguarding of dangerous waters with lifebuoys, and the distribution of metal posters showing the latest methods of resuscitation in cases of drowning, gas poisoning and electric shock.

From its inception in 1785 to the present day, the Society has rewarded acts of heroism in saving others from death, on land or sea, with gold, silver and bronze medals, and certificates. In its list of nearly three thousand names may be found gallant stories of sacrifice by old and young, the running of risks fraught with imminent danger, and in many cases the giving up of life itself that others might survive.

All in all, perhaps few organizations in the world can furnish more records of the spirit of courage, of enterprise, and of unselfish devotion, than will be found in the long and honorable history of the Humane Society of the Commonwealth of Massachusetts.

★

Exhibits

NANTUCKET — *Whaling Museum.* For nearly two centuries Nantucket was the leading whaling port of the world; her citizens were almost entirely dependent on the whaling industry, and her ships were to be found on every ocean. In the Nantucket Whaling Museum are preserved the relics and traditions of those days. Here is exhibited one of the largest and best collections of whaling implements and material, including harpoons and lances purchased in Hull, England, and which were taken from Nantucket whaleships captured by British privateers during the American Revolution.

The Museum is housed in a large brick house built in 1847 and operated as a sperm candle manufactory. It is located at the head of Steamboat Wharf.

Nantucket is reached from South Station (Boston) by train to Woods Hole and from there by daily steamers to the island. The Nantucket Whaling Museum is open week days from 9 to 6 and probably on Sundays from 2 to 6. There is a charge of 25¢. for admission.

PROVINCETOWN — *Historical Museum.* In the Provincetown Museum is a marine collection consisting of the model of a whaler, implements of whaling, scrimshaw work, a gun carriage washed ashore at Provincetown during the war of 1812, and various exhibitions of drying fish. In addition, the arctic collection of Donald B. MacMillan is displayed.

The Historical Museum is open daily from 9 to 6 and on Sundays from 10 to 5. Admission charge is 25¢. Provincetown may be reached by train from the South Station (Boston) or by a daily excursion boat from Long Wharf, on Atlantic Avenue.

THE SHIPWRECKED BARQUE "SALUTE"

PLYMOUTH AND DUXBURY — Plymouth Rock is the object one naturally seeks when visiting Plymouth. In Pilgrim Hall are numerous mementos of the Pilgrims, including personal belongings of the Mayflower passengers.

A few miles to the north of Plymouth is Duxbury, which was named after Duxborough Hall, the ancestral home of Miles Standish. Duxbury was allotted to John Alden, the youngest of the Pilgrims, and his house still stands, and is open to visitors.

Miles Standish lived in Duxbury because he felt Plymouth to be too crowded for comfortable living. Today Duxbury is the second largest yachting center on the east coast of the United States.

Plymouth and Duxbury may be reached by train from the South Station or by daily boat (except Mondays) from Rowes Wharf on Atlantic Avenue (Boston) to Plymouth.

SOUTH DARTMOUTH — *The whaleship "Charles W. Morgan."* On the estate of Colonel E. H. R. Green the whaleship *"Charles W. Morgan"* is permanently moored beside a wharf. Her hull is embedded in concrete so that she makes a lasting exhibit of a real whaler. The *Charles W. Morgan* was launched at New Bedford in 1841 and has seen many years of actual whaling. She has her full equipment, including one whaleboat which was broken in taking a whale. She makes a most unusual and interesting spectacle well worth the short trip out from New Bedford.

The vessel is open for inspection from 9 to 6. There is no charge for admission. New Bedford may be reached by train from the South Station (Boston) and South Dartmouth by automobile from New Bedford.

NEW BEDFORD — *Old Dartmouth Historical Society and Whaling Museum.* New Bedford supplanted Nantucket as the leading whaling port of the world when the larger whaling vessels became common, and the bar before Nantucket's harbor limited the draft of vessels entering that port.

A remarkable tribute to New Bedford's maritime greatness is exhibited in the Whaling Museum. Chief among the exhibits is a half-sized model of the whaleship *Lagoda*. This bark is complete in every detail. She is housed in a separate building (the Bourne Building) and is large enough for visitors to board and go below.

In constructing the model great care was taken to search out whalemen and artisans who had worked on the actual *Lagoda*, and her equipment of boats and sails has been made by local firms who have survived the all but extinct whaling industry.

In the same building with the *Lagoda* are exhibited models of various types of sailing craft and a large collection of whaling irons. In the gallery have been constructed replicas of old-time shops which were characteristic of New Bedford when whaling was at its height. Among these are a ship agent's office, a sail loft, a cooper's shop, a shipsmith's shop, a rigging loft and a whaleboat shop.

In another building (the Rogers Building) is a section devoted to marine exhibits. Here may be seen two large and elaborate "dockyard" models of old ships. Here also is a display of ship pictures, many examples of scrimshaw work and a large collection of the logs of New Bedford vessels.

The Dartmouth Museum is open from 9 to 5 except Sundays and holidays. The admission charge is 25¢.

NEWBURYPORT — Newburyport, on the Merrimac River, is one of the famous old-time Massachusetts ports. In its Marine Museum is a collection of curiosities brought home by the ships of Newburyport, and numerous ship models. Here is located the mansion of "Lord" Timothy Dexter, the eccentric merchant who made his large fortune by unusual ventures, such as sending a cargo of warming-pans to the West Indies and profitably disposing of them there.

Newburyport may be reached by train from North Station (Boston).

GLOUCESTER—*Fisheries.*—For over three hundred years the Fisheries have been carried on from the Port of Gloucester. There are today over one hundred and sixty Gloucester fishing vessels actively engaged in the industry.

Real romance of the sea is to be found at Gloucester. A visitor to the waterfront may see vessels coming in to the different wharves to unload their catches; others tied up preparing for another trip, with sails hanging loosely to dry; fishermen overhauling fish gear, mending nets, baiting up; here and there an artist—for many artists make their homes at Gloucester during the summer time, transferring to canvas all this activity—and vessels slipping quietly away from their docks, heading for the outer harbor, out and beyond the breakwater to sea, to return when they have made their catch.

A visit should be made to the fish canning and fish packing plants where different fish products are manufactured; to the fillet factories where whole slices of fresh fishmeat are prepared and frosted; and to the fish drying flakes where thousands of pounds of fish are dried and cured by the sun's rays.

"CHARLES W. MORGAN"
Now permanently preserved as "Whaling Enshrined" at South Dartmouth

It is worth much to chat with some of the fishermen along the waterfront. Many a thrilling story of the sea is to be heard—stories of heroism or of romance, not of themselves but of their dory mates; and they may tell of some of the Gloucester men who have gone down with their ships and for whom the City has erected the Fisherman's Permanent Memorial on the Boulevard facing the harbor.

The people of Gloucester and those associated in her Fisheries extend a cordial welcome to visitors. The Chamber of Commerce will furnish information as to which points are of especial interest and advise where guides may be obtained.

SALEM — *Peabody Museum.* This museum originated as the Salem East India Marine Society in 1799 which was founded "to assist the widows and children of its members," for the collection of material for the improvement of navigation, and to form a museum of curiosities. Its membership was restricted to "any persons who shall have navigated the seas near the Cape of Good Hope or Cape Horn either as Master or Commander or (being of the age of twenty-one years) as Factor or Supercargo of any vessel belonging to Salem."

The Peabody Museum is housed in an interesting old granite-faced brick building and contains one of the most extensive collections of ship models, ship pictures, and marine relics in the country. On the upper floors are a natural history collection and an extensive ethnological collection especially rich in objects illustrating the culture of old Japan, Hawaii, and the South Sea Islands.

In the marine exhibition is a whaling collection, including actual whaling irons, products of the industry, models of whaling vessels, and many souvenirs made on long voyages by the sailors.

In another room is an unusual collection of early navigating instruments, including some which once belonged to Nathaniel Bowditch. The walls of this room are covered with rare ship pictures and portraits of Salem merchants and shipmasters who helped make Salem prosperous.

Among the many excellent and complete ship models is one of the *"Constitution"* given by Captain Isaac Hull to the museum when he was fresh from the capture of the *"Guerrière."* This model was followed in rigging *"Old Ironsides"* in 1907 when she was restored by order of Congress.

The Peabody Museum is open from 9 to 5 on week days and 2 to 5 on

Sundays. There is no charge for admission. Salem may be reached by trains from the North Station (Boston).

MARBLEHEAD — In 1775 Marblehead was second only to Boston in population, and was of outstanding importance in the American Revolution. A full regiment was made up there for the Continental Army, and to this regiment, called the "amphibians," was entrusted the ferrying of Washington's troops across the East River after its defeat on Lond Island. A large part of the crew of the *Constitution* enlisted from Marblehead, and it was the home port of many of the most famous Massachusetts privateers. Today it is the largest yachting center on the east coast of the United States.

Marblehead may be reached by train from the North Station (Boston).

BOSTON — *Boston Fish Pier*. The fishing industry to which Massachusetts owes so much is still continued on a vast scale in Boston, at the Fish Pier. Here are handled three hundred million pounds of fish and sea food each year.

Boston Fish Pier is a large modern pier around which cluster the fishing vessels—sail and power—often two and three deep. Here a visitor may watch the vessels come in, see their cargoes auctioned off on the Exchange, watch the fish unloaded and transported by modern conveyors through the largest ice plant in New England, and the frozen fish finally stacked up like cordwood in the cold storage rooms. In other smaller manufacturing units the fish are cut in fillets to be sold fresh and unfrozen: along the shore-line are the stores of the large dealers in shell-fish and oysters; and everywhere is the atmosphere of this old-time industry, now on a modern footing with its power trawlers and fish handling machinery.

The Pier makes a spectacle well worth seeing, and a visit on a hot day to a freezing room twenty degrees below zero is attractive. The early morning is usually the most interesting time.

Boston Fish Pier may be reached from the South Station by trolley (Summer Street Extension) or by bus. Visitors should ask for the office of the Massachusetts Fisheries Association where guides will be provided.

The Fish Pier is open from 7.30 to 5.00 week days. There is no charge for admission.

BOSTON — *Marine Museum*. In the Old State House built in 1747 at the head of State Street (formerly Queen Street) is the Marine Museum.

Courtesy of Society for the Preservation of New England Antiquities.

U.S.S. CONSTITUTION

This was the second Town House, as the original, built in 1657, was destroyed by fire.

The Marine Museum occupies half of the lower story, and contains numerous ship models ranging from an excellent admiralty model of an English ship to a more modern model of a sealer, showing the process of collecting seals. One of the two remarkably fine models of the *Constitution* built by Lieutenant Colonel Spicer is in this collection. Ship pictures, whaling gear, scrimshaw work and marine relics are also displayed. There is no charge for admission. The Marine Museum is open from 9 to 4 except Sundays.

BOSTON — *Museum of Fine Arts* on Huntington Avenue. Here is exhibited a loan collection of ship models including Lieutenant Colonel Spicer's last model of the *Constitution*. There is no charge for admission. The Museum of Fine Arts is open from 10 to 5 on week days, except Mondays, and on Sundays from 1 to 5.

BOSTON — *State Street Trust Company*. In the State Street Trust Company the banking rooms have been patterned after an old-time counting house, and a visitor is greeted on all sides with interesting curios.

Particularly of marine interest are the many models of privateers, merchant ships and whalers mounted on the grill work and throughout the bank. Just inside the entrance is an excellent and complete model of a privateer, made entirely by the people of the bank. On the walls are many ship and marine pictures, most of them rare.

BOSTON (Charlestown) *Navy Yard*. This yard, which was established in 1800, is one of the oldest in the country. Here may be seen a variety of war vessels, either in the water or drydock. The rope-walk manufactures rope for the entire navy, and is now making, from American hemp, the cordage for the *Constitution*.

The most distinguished exhibit in the country is the *Constitution* at the Navy Yard. Under the direction of Lieutenant John A. Lord she has been wholly rebuilt, was relaunched in May, and will still be under construction for another year.

Her spars and rigging will not be completed this summer, but most of the reconstruction on her hull is done, and visitors may board her and visit many parts of the ship.

A visit to the *Constitution* is tremendously worth while, and is, moreover, one of the easiest exhibits to reach. Take the Boston Elevated (Forest Hills-Everett Line) to City Square, Charlestown, and walk three blocks to the Navy Yard. The Navy Yard is open every day from 9.00 to 4.30. There is no admission charge.

U. S. S. Constitution*

IN THE YEAR 1785 the Algerian Corsairs of the Mediterranean captured two United States merchant vessels whose crews were made
slaves, and $59,496 demanded for their ransom. Although this was a
clear case of piracy the young United States was unable to exact repara-
tion, and negotiations for the payment of this ransom were begun. In
1793 eleven more American vessels were taken by the Algerians yet even
this degradation stirred only a bare majority of Congress. However, it
was decided to build six frigates, of which three, the *Constitution*, the
Constellation and the *United States* were first completed. They were the
foundation of the United States Navy.

Mr. Joshua Humphreys, a well known shipbuilder of Philadelphia, was
chosen as designer of the vessels. The hull of the *Constitution* was modeled
after the best French naval practice, having finer lines than were common
in England. Her sides noticeably "tumbled home," or sloped inward,
making the upper deck narrower than the deck below, to ease her motion
in a seaway. She was as heavily built as a line-of-battle ship though
rated only as a frigate. Her ribs of live oak were placed less than two
inches apart which, with her inner and outer planking, made her sides
nearly twenty-two inches thick. She was heavily sparred. Her above-water
lines did not promise particular speed yet she proved to be such an
advance in design that she and her sister ships eventually revolutionized
the design of foreign war vessels.

The *Constitution* was built in Hartt's Naval Yard in Boston near what
is now Constitution Wharf on Atlantic Avenue. Her anchors came from
Hanover, Mass., her sails were made in the old Granary Building at the
corner of Park and Tremont Streets, and Paul Revere furnished the
copper bolts for her hull. Her construction was well along by 1795 when a
debasing treaty was signed with Algiers, paying them over a million
dollars for the redemption of captives. Congress thereupon reconsidered
the advisability of spending money for a navy and decided to rush the
work on those three frigates, which were nearest completion.

Her launching in 1797 was rather inauspicious, as she stuck on the ways

* With acknowledgment to the *Frigate Constitution*, by Ira N. Hollis. By permission of Houghton Mifflin
Company.

and a month's work was required to get her into the water. The money for equipping her was not appropriated for another year, and she commenced her first cruise, which was among the Windward Islands, in July 1798. In 1801 she was recalled to the Boston Navy Yard and lay there dismantled for two years. In 1803 under command of Edward Preble the *Constitution*, again in commission, sailed for the Barbary Coast to break the power of the corsair.

Our treaty and indemnity with Algiers had encouraged the cupidity of Tripoli whose Dey demanded the gift of a frigate. Decisive action was clearly needed. With the *Constitution* as flagship, six vessels including the ill-fated frigate *Philadelphia*, and five small schooners and brigs commenced a blockade of Tripoli,—a particularly difficult task, as prevailing winds tended to drive the vessels onto a lee shore.

The capture of the *Philadelphia* by the pirates and her destruction under the guns of the harbor forts by Decatur, the heroic sacrifice of Somers on the *Intrepid*, the devotion of every man in the American squadron through two years of wearisome blockade duty, and the ultimate humbling of the Dey in 1805 are oft-told tales. The *Constitution* was the backbone of the successful enterprise which cast in unfavorable light the long submission of Europe to the piracies of Tripoli.

The prelude to the War of 1812 with England was the episode of the *Chesapeake*. Our warship, the *Chesapeake*, outward bound for the Mediterranean, was stopped by the British ship *Leopard* which proposed to search her for deserters. The Captain of the *Chesapeake* had not cleared his ship for action, and delayed an answer to gain time. The English commander did not wait for a reply, but fired several broadsides into the *Chesapeake* until she surrendered; then the American crew were mustered on deck and four men removed.

Relations with England, largely on account of impressing seamen, became more and more strained until war was declared in 1812.

To declare war against England at this time seemed a foolhardy act. England controlled the seas. She had between six and seven hundred armed vessels afloat while we had but twenty ships in fighting trim. More than this was the English Navy's long standing record of victory, and its supreme confidence. We were untried, while the thought of defeat never even occurred to them. On the other hand, the spirit of American seamen was high. They were willing and quick to learn gunnery,—an

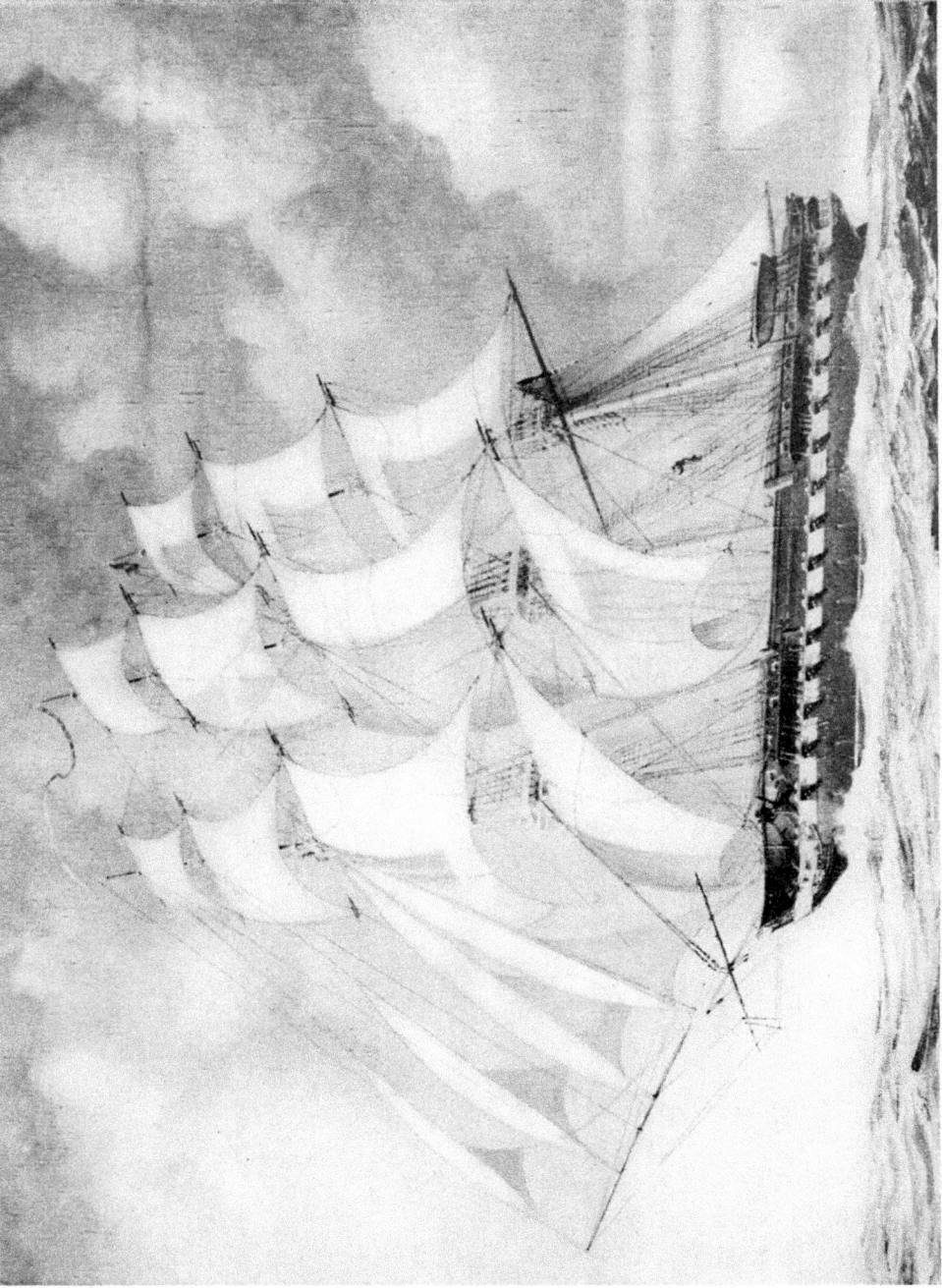

Courtesy of T. M. Prudden.

U.S.S. CONSTITUTION

Painting by Henry W. Moore.

outstanding advantage throughout the war,—and our officers made an intelligent study of tactics while the English still labored under the traditions of Nelson who ordered "Never mind manoeuvers, always go at them."

The *Constitution* put to sea three days after the declaration of war under command of Isaac Hull, and unexpectedly met a British squadron consisting of the *Guerrière* and two other warships. When the wind failed she was kept ahead of her pursuers by her usual good luck and by the ingenuity of Captain Hull through kedging, which was the carrying of an anchor ahead and hauling the ship forward while a second anchor was carried still further ahead to repeat the operation. On this occasion she narrowly escaped capture.

A few months later while cruising off the Grand Banks she again met the *Guerrière*, this time alone. Both ships cleared for action, and for three-quarters of an hour an inconclusive battle raged. Hull reserved the fire of many of his guns, awaiting just the right moment when his whole broadside would be effective. The moment came when the two vessels were sailing on the same tack with the *Constitution* to windward, over-hauling the *Guerrière*. Both opened a heavy fire. In ten minutes the enemy's mizzen-mast fell over the side, knocking a large hole in her counter. The *Constitution* forged ahead, crossing the *Guerrière's* bows, and fired two raking broadsides which did fearful damage. The *Constitution* meanwhile received a shot in her cabin which set her afire. This blaze was extinguished, but the jibboom of the *Guerrière* had fouled in the rigging of the *Constitution* and it looked as though the Britishers were preparing to board.

As the *Constitution* wore around, the foremast and mainmast of the enemy were carried away, leaving her a hopeless wreck, and she surrendered. The prisoners were transferred to the victor, and the *Guerrière* set afire. It was in this action that an American seaman noticed an English cannon ball rebound from the side of the *Constitution* and is said to have called "Huzza, her sides are made of iron!", hence the term "Old Ironsides."

The effect of the victory was tremendous. The land operations of the war had not been successful. New England was openly talking secession, when our infant navy from which little had been expected furnished a bright ray of hope in the gloomy scene. The *Constitution* returned to Boston and the city exulted.

A brief overhaul, and the *Constitution* put to sea under Commodore Bainbridge, the man who had commanded the *Philadelphia* at the time of her stranding and capture off Tripoli. Two months later, off the coast of Brazil, she sighted the British man-o-war *Java* conveying a captured American merchantman. The vessels closed on each other and a vigorous action ensued, both manoeuvering for the weather gauge. The *Java* was the faster ship and three times endeavored to cross the *Constitution's* bows, to rake her. This was avoided, for the American ship was remarkably well handled. The *Java* lost her bowsprit and jibboom which so handicapped her that extreme measures seemed advisable. Captain Lambert of the *Java* therefore tried to lay her alongside to board but lost his foremast in so doing. The musketry from the top of the American vessel was particularly effective, as was all the American gunnery, and far superior to the English. Captain Lambert was fatally wounded. The steering wheel of the *Constitution* was carried away, but the battle had continued for less than an hour before every spar of the *Java* had fallen except part of her mainmast. The wreckage so littered her decks that the guns could not be handled, and she struck her colors. The *Constitution* suffered somewhat in her rigging and masts but not enough to prevent her making the long voyage back to Boston a week later. The English ship was blown up, as she was unseaworthy. From quite conflicting testimony it seems probable that the *Java* carried about as many men as the *Constitution*, but nearly five times as many were killed and wounded on her as on her adversary.

She was the third frigate lost by the British within five months and her destruction caused consternation. The contempt of England for our navy was turned to respect. These victories, moreover, reawakened the interest of Congress in an American navy, and four line-of-battle ships and six more frigates were authorized.

At the Boston Navy Yard the *Constitution* was overhauled and the damage caused by the *Java* repaired. Shortly after putting to sea again, under Captain Charles Stewart, she met two English frigates off Portsmouth. The wind died away and she was in great danger of capture; only by masterful seamanship and the throwing overboard of everything that could be spared to lighten her was she safely worked into Marblehead under the guns of Fort Sewall. Not only were prize goods thrown overboard, but the spirit tanks were emptied to lessen her burden. It is interesting to note that enough rum was carried in those days to make this

LEVANT   CONSTITUTION   CYANE

View of the action between the U.S. Frigate Constitution & the British Ships Levant & Cyane

Courtesy of Peabody Museum of Salem.

sacrifice worth while. From Marblehead the *Constitution* slipped down to Boston where she was bottled up for eight months.

A break in the blockade allowed her to escape from port, and she cruised off Portugal. Here Captain Stewart learned that peace had been declared, but not having been officially notified, he continued the capture of such small English vessels as he met.

This cruise, however, was disappointing, and the *Constitution* started for home. Near the Madeiras she sighted the British frigate *Cyane* in company with the ship *Levant*. The American frigate bore down on both vessels, but lost her main royal-mast. Without stopping the chase a new mast was sent up,—a tricky operation at best even when lying quietly in the wind. She caught up with the enemy, and for an hour an ineffectual sparring match ensued, the British ship trying vainly to get to windward, and apparently hoping to postpone the action till darkness. The vessels closed on each other, and a short hot action followed. The *Constitution* found herself abreast of the *Levant*, fired her broadside, and under cover of the dense masses of smoke braced her yards back and instead of forging ahead as her adversary expected, sailed astern to pour her fire at the *Cyane*. Sailing a ship backward in these days of fore-n-aft rigged vessels is unknown but it was common in the times of square riggers. Again filling her sails, the American ship bore down on the *Levant*, firing two broadsides which so badly damaged her that she withdrew from the fight. Then the *Constitution* passed under the stern of the *Cyane* and gave her a raking fire down her deck. The *Cyane's* case was hopeless, she was badly hulled and her main and mizzen-masts were in danger of falling, so a light was hoisted in token of surrender, the battle having been fought mostly by moonlight.

The *Levant* meanwhile having repaired some of the damage to her rigging, and not realizing that her consort had struck, returned to the fight. The *Constitution* repeated her manoeuver of passing under the stern of the British ship and raking her. The *Levant's* wheel was shot away and she tried to run, but, after a short chase, surrendered.

This was the last great fight of the *Constitution*, and although she fought alone against two ships the odds were in her favor. The total number of guns of the British vessels was fully equal to that of the American, but they were lighter and capable of inflicting less damage. The crews of the two enemy vessels numbered 320 as against 457 men on the *Constitution*.

Captain Stewart took his prizes to the Cape Verde Islands where he met a squadron of three British men-of-war. The American convoy split, and the enemy fortunately centered their chase on the *Levant* which they retook, but in so doing permitted the escape and return to New York of both the *Cyane* and her captor.

The *Constitution* was not the only American frigate which was effective in the War of 1812, but she was by far the most successful, and was responsible for more than half the number of guns captured.

She was again overhauled, and lay at her dock in Boston for six years. In 1823 she sailed for the Mediterranean on a cruise that lasted nearly four years. It was between 1828 and 1830 that she was surveyed at the Boston Navy Yard and reported to be so unsound and badly decayed that the expense of repairs would be greater than her original cost. She would have been broken up had not Oliver Wendell Holmes stirred the whole Country by his famous poem "Old Ironsides." Congress appropriated the money to rebuild her and she virtually became a new ship.

This work was completed at the time of Andrew Jackson's enthusiastic reception in Boston, and the commandant of the Navy Yard thought he was gratifying public opinion by placing a figurehead of Andrew Jackson on the bow of the rebuilt frigate, to replace the original figurehead of Hercules which had been shot away at Tripoli. Unfortunately the well-intended idea aroused a storm of indignation and resulted in an aspiring youth rowing out to the frigate as she lay at anchor during a thunder-storm, sawing off Andrew Jackson's head, and returning with it as a trophy. Both the head and the body are now at the Naval Academy.

In the following twenty years the *Constitution* cruised in the Mediterranean, off the coast of South America and in the China Seas, until 1855 when she went out of commission at Portsmouth, never again to be used in active service. In 1860 she was moved to the Naval Academy to become a training ship. During the Civil War threats of capture, as had befallen her sister ship the *United States*, caused her to be towed to the New York Navy Yard. By 1871 she was in too poor condition to be trusted under sail at sea, and for a second time was in danger of being broken up. Instead, she was restored at the Philadelphia Navy Yard, and in 1874 and 1878 made two voyages to Europe to transport exhibits to the exposition at Paris, and as a naval training ship. For a short time she lay at New York, then in 1883, became a receiving ship at the Navy

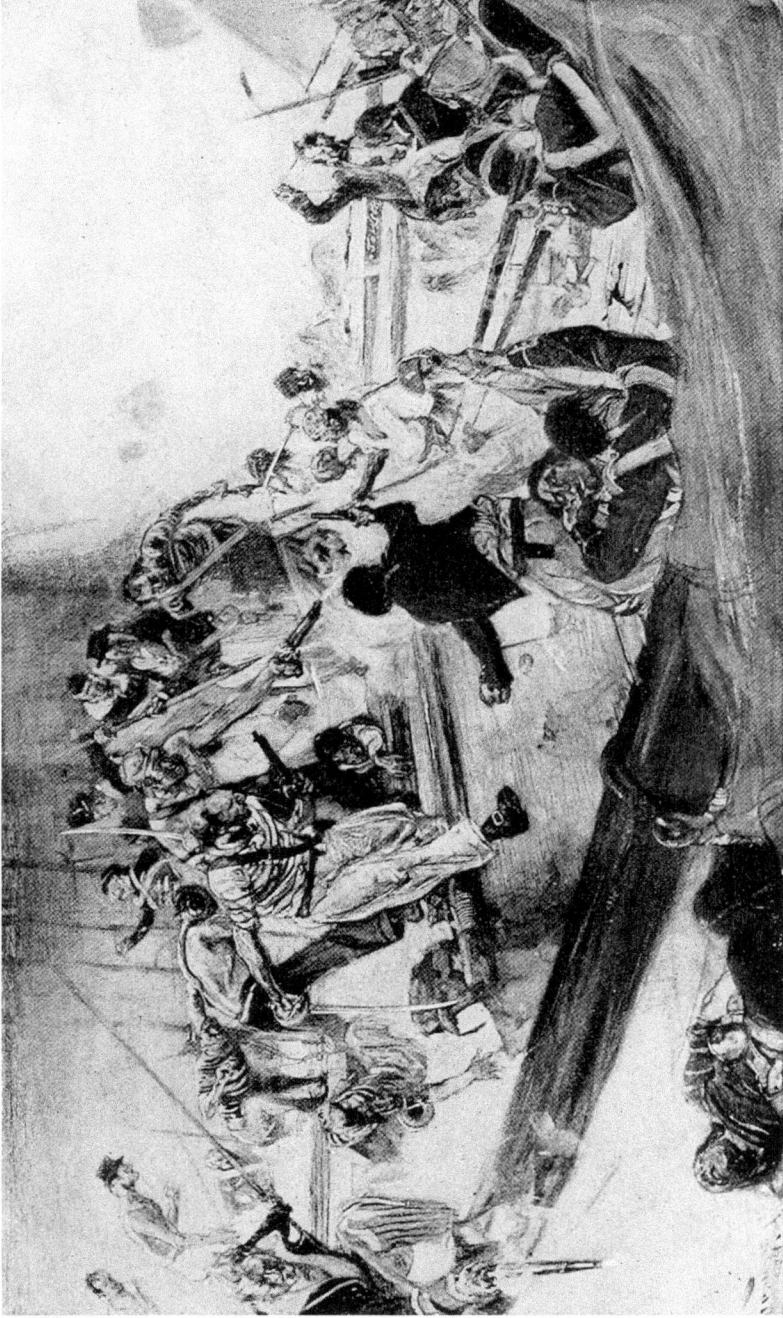

From a drawing by Henry Reuterdahl, copyright Scribner's Magazine.

A NAVAL ENGAGEMENT OF 1812

Yard at Kittery, Maine. In 1897, on the hundredth anniversary of her launching, she was towed back to Boston.

* * * * * * * * * * * *

This brief history would not be complete without an acknowledgment to Admiral Philip Andrews whose devotion and energy in sustaining popular interest in the *Constitution* made her reconstruction possible.

Upon the completion of the National Save Old Ironsides Campaign, approximately $645,000 was available for work on the ship. Profits from the sale of lithographed pictures brought in $165,000. Profits from the sale of souvenirs, made from wood and metal removed from the original hull of the ship during her rebuilding, amounted to $126,000. Interest on bank deposits of $28,000 was credited to the fund. Of the $326,000 received as donations, the school children of the United States contributed the amount of $155,000.

Lieutenant John A. Lord, Naval Constructor, reported in connection with the rebuilding of the *Constitution* in 1925. For two years he devoted his time to research and making plans to restore the old frigate as she was in the days of 1812.

The undertaking was enormous, in view of the scarcity of correct information. It was necessary to visit the old shipbuilding centers from Maine to Florida in order to find workmen sufficiently skilled in the rapidly disappearing art of building wooden ships. To obtain proper material for the oak knees, spars, and heavy keel timbers, he was obliged to draw on all sections of the country, including the tall pine forests of the Northwest.

When the work of restoration began in April 1927, Lieutenant Lord took charge, and has superintended every detail of its prosecution. When the task is completed, about June 1, 1931, the frigate will be better built, stronger, and more lasting than when first launched one hundred thirty-three years ago. To Lieutenant Lord we shall owe a debt of gratitude that this gallant old ship, entirely seaworthy, fully rigged and equipped as in the days of 1812, will be ready to visit all our principal ports.

* * * * * * * * * * * *

"Our Declaration of Independence," it has been said, "was only a declaration. The United States did not really gain independence until the

War of 1812. The battles of the *Constitution* made this independence an accomplished fact."

She is more than an old-time ship preserved as a relic of the past. Our champion in battle against piracy and oppression, her victories inspired national confidence in crises when confidence was needed. When she was launched in 1797, we were an experiment among the governments of men. She lives as an emblem of the years and deeds she has seen.

★

PROGRAM

OF

MARINE EVENTS

OF MASSACHUSETTS

SUMMER

1930

★

Published by

TERCENTENARY MARINE COMMITTEE

The office of the TERCENTENARY MARINE COMMITTEE is at 22 Beacon Street, Boston.
(Telephone Haymarket 6414.) It is open from 9:00 A.M. until 5:00 P.M. and our
staff will endeavor to furnish information pertaining to the marine
celebrations throughout the summer.

List of Boat Landings on Boston Waterfront

PUBLIC LANDINGS

Northern Avenue Bridge (below bridge). Float about 30 feet long, 20 feet wide.
Summer Street Bridge next to South Station. Float about 30 feet long, 20 feet wide.
City Point between head house and South Boston Yacht Club, Warren Bridge. Float about 40 feet long, 20 feet wide.

PRIVATE LANDINGS

Noyes-Buick float; South Boston side Fort Point Channel, near Summer Street, between Summer and Congress Street bridges.
Boston Yacht Club—Small float at Rowes Wharf (now being repaired).
South Boston Yacht Club—Float at City Point.
Columbia Yacht Club   —Float at City Point.
Boston Yacht Club   —Float at City Point.
Chelsea Yacht Club   —Float at North Mystic Bridge.
Bunke. Hill Yacht Club   —Float at Little Mystic.
Jeffries Point   —Float at East Boston near Air Port.

Schedule of Steamboat Trips from Boston

NEW YORK—Eastern Steamship Company, India Wharf, Atlantic Avenue. The boat sails daily at 5:00 P.M. (daylight saving time), and takes the course through the Cape Cod Canal.

BANGOR, MAINE—Eastern Steamship Company, India Wharf, Atlantic Avenue. Daily sailings at 6:00 P.M. (daylight saving time) after June 29th.

YARMOUTH, NOVA SCOTIA.—Eastern Steamship Company, Central Wharf, Atlantic Avenue. Daily sailings, except Saturdays, at 3:00 P.M. (daylight saving time) after June 29th.

PROVINCETOWN, MASS.—Cape Cod Steamship Company, Long Wharf, Atlantic Avenue. This is an all day, round trip with two hours stay at Provincetown. The boat sails weekdays at 9.30 A.M. (daylight saving time) and is back the same day at 7.30 P.M. On Sundays it sails at 10:00 A.M. and is back at 8:00 P.M.

NANTASKET, MASS.—Nantasket Beach Steamboat Company, Rowe's Wharf, Atlantic Avenue. Excursion steamers sail nearly every hour starting at 7.15 A.M. (daylight saving time) and until 11:15 P.M. The round trip takes a little over two hours.

PLYMOUTH, MASS.—Nantasket Beach Steamboat Company, Rowe's Wharf, Atlantic Avenue. This is an all day sail leaving at 10:00 A.M. (daylight saving time) on Sunday, Tuesday, Wednesday, Thursday and Friday, docking at Boston at 6:30 P.M. On Saturday the boat leaves at 2:00 P.M. and docks at Boston at 10:00 P.M. The 2½-hour stay in Plymouth permits an excursion through the town.

BOSTON HARBOR—Nantasket Beach Steamboat Company, Rowe's Wharf, Atlantic Avenue. The steamer *Mayflower* sails every evening except Sunday and Monday at 8:30 P.M. (daylight saving time) for a harbor sail and dancing. She docks again at 11:00 P.M. but the dancing continues until 12:00 P.M.

BOSTON HARBOR—Fishing Trip. King Philip Steamboat Company, No. 25 T Wharf, Atlantic Avenue. Telephone Richmond 3374. The *King Philip* sails daily at 10:00 A.M. (daylight saving time) for an all day fishing trip outside of Boston Harbor, and including a brief sightseeing tour of the harbor. She docks at 5:15 P.M. All fishing gear is provided, as well as chowder.

BOSTON HARBOR—Evening Harbor Sail. King Philip Steamboat Company, No. 25 T Wharf, Atlantic Avenue. Telephone Richmond 3374. After July 1st, the *King Philip* will sail every evening except Sunday at 8:45 (daylight saving time) for a harbor sail, and dancing, and will dock at 11:20 P.M.

Program of

Marine Events

June 7

DORCHESTER DAY. Yacht Races.

June 12

SALEM. Reenactment of the arrival in 1630 of the Ship Arbella carrying Governor John Winthrop with charter and government of the Colony. The Arbella has been reproduced for this event, but she will be exhibited at other ports and eventually in the Charles River Basin. Guide service from Salem Chamber of Commerce at Hotel Hawthorne.

June 15

NANTUCKET. Informal opening of the new Whaling Museum.

June 23, 24, 25

OFF NEWPORT, R. I. Three day races off Newport of the *Enterprise*, *Weetamoe*, *Whirlwind* and *Yankee*, the four yachts from which one will be selected to defend the *America's* cup, together with the *Resolute*, which defended the *America's* cup in the last International Races, and the *Vanitie* which competed with the *Resolute* at that time for the privilege of defending the cup. This event will be under the auspices of the Eastern Yacht Club, and will be the best test of the season of the four new boats against the two old ones.

June 27

BOSTON. Welcome home to Admiral Byrd from the Antarctic.

July 4

FALL RIVER (Touisset). First yacht races of the summer series. The classes contending will be Warwick Neck class (7 entries) and Candy class (9 entries). Tercentenary Trophies will be awarded.

July 6, 7, 8, 9

NEWBURYPORT. Reception and dancing—visits to warships in harbor, sports, aviation events. Guide service for visitors.

July 7, 8, 9, 10, 11, 12, 14, 15, 16, 17, 18, 19

OFF NEWPORT, R. I. Observation races held for the four new contenders to defend the *America's* cup in September. In these races the New York Yacht Club Race Committee will form opinions on the relative merits of the four boats.

July 12

QUINCY. Motor boat races.—Seven races with two heats in each race.
Tercentenary Trophies will be awarded.
These races may be viewed from the boulevard which skirts the Wollaston shore.

July 13

HINGHAM. Yacht races for Tercentenary Trophies. Two classes, O-boats (17 contestants) and Mighty Mites. These races will be held at 3.00 P.M. by the Hingham Yacht Club, who extend the courtesies of their club to visitors for this afternoon.

July 15

BOSTON. The Great Meeting. Prominent guests and speakers including the President, and Governors of various States. The incompleted *U.S.S. Constitution* will be on display at the Navy Yard, as well as United States light cruisers and foreign war vessels.

July 20

QUINCY. Sailing races under the auspices of the Squantum, Quincy and Wollaston Yacht Clubs for Tercentenary Trophies. There will be nine classes of boats and from five to thirty-five boats in each class. These races may be viewed from the boulevard which skirts the Wollaston shore.

July 27

BOSTON. Boston Harbor and Massachusetts Bay combined yacht club races, water parade and illumination (contributed by the Tercentenary Marine Committee).
Tercentenary Trophies will be awarded.

July 31–*August* 1–2

BOSTON (Charles River Basin). National regatta of rowing races, illumination and fireworks (provided by the Tercentenary Marine Committee). This regatta is under the auspices of the National Association of Amateur Oarsmen and will comprise 8-oar, 4-oar and single races, a woman's ¼ mile dash, a junior eight-oared race, an octuple race, and a war canoe race, besides cutter races for naval and coast guard crews. For the first time in seventeen years this regatta, which is made up of boat clubs from all parts of the country, will be rowed in Boston.
Tercentenary Medals will be awarded.

August 2

GLOUCESTER (Eastern Point). Tercentenary Trophies will be presented to the leading boats at the end of the first series regatta of the Eastern Point Yacht Club. The Classes contesting will be Sonder boats (14 entries) Triangles (14 entries), and Cape Cod knockabouts (14 entries).

PROVINCETOWN (date not determined). Yacht races for Tercentenary Trophies (eight 23 foot one-design knockabouts). Yacht club quarters on the upper floor of the Board of Trade building will be open to visitors. (Call office of Marine Committee for date.)

August 2

EDGARTOWN (Martha's Vineyard). The Edgartown Yacht Club will hold its seventh annual regatta in which will participate nearly 140 yachts from 8 nearby yacht clubs. Among the 18 classes contesting will be Wianno knockabouts, Vineyard Sound interclub classes, Indian class, 15 foot knockabouts, Katama class and perhaps the Herreshoff S class from New Bedford and the O boats from Nonquit. In addition there will be handicap races for schooners and ketches, and for sloops and yawls.
    Tercentenary Trophies will be awarded.

August 9–16

MARBLEHEAD (Marblehead Week). Yacht racing each day. On Wednesday the 13th the races will be under the auspices of Boston Yacht Club and Tercentenary Trophies will be given in all classes of yachts (perhaps 30).
    This is the largest and most important regatta of the season.

August 12

WALTHAM (Evening). Charles River water carnival, canoe pageant and illumination.

ANNISQUAM (date not determined). Sailing regatta for Tercentenary Trophies. In these races it is expected the Gloucester Yacht Club will join, making entries as follows:—Class R (9 boats), Triangle class (11 boats) T-15 footers (4 boats), Bird class (5 boats), catboats (18 boats), Fish class (16 boats). The Annisquam Yacht Club will extend the privileges of its house to visitors during this regatta. (Call office of Marine Committee for date.)

August 13

NANTUCKET. Yacht regatta and whale-boat races.

August 13, 14, 15, 16

DUXBURY. Sailing regatta for Tercentenary Trophies on three days at 1.00. 1.30, 2.15 and 3.00 o'clock respectively. In these races the Pilgrim Yacht Club of Plymouth will join, bringing their Duck class of knockabouts. The classes racing will be Pilgrim class (5 boats) 15 foot knockabouts (4 boats) Ducks (40 to 50 boats) and 15 foot catboats (6 boats).

August 20, 21, 22, 23, 25, 26, 27, 28, 29, 30

OFF NEWPORT. The *Enterprise, Weetamoe, Whirlwind,* and *Yankee* will race, and the New York Yacht Club Race Committee will select the one best fitted to defend the *America's cup.*

August 30–31—September 1

WINTHROP. Three day sailing regatta. The classes will be Class I (10 boats), Indian (20 boats), Cottage Park 17's (7 boats), Quincy Cats, Winthrop 15's Winthrop Hustlers and Snowbirds. There will also be outboard motor races, in five classes.

Tercentenary Trophies will be awarded.

September 6

MANCHESTER. The 1930 Jeffrey's Ledge Race of the Cruising Club of America. This is an annual ocean race for auxiliary cruising boats of not over sixty-five feet over all length. For a number of years similar races have been sailed, and so far no start has been postponed on account of weather. Twenty or more boats will enter; the contest being open to both members and non-members. There is no entry fee, but all boats must comply with the Committee's standards of seaworthiness and must carry prescribed equipment. No paid hands are permitted. A small gasoline allowance, and handicaps for size and rig make this 138 mile race, in which many of the ablest cruising men of these waters compete, a close and interesting event. Handicaps are given at the start so that in each class the first boat to finish wins. The first boat will start at seven o'clock (daylight saving time), the others starting later according to their handicaps. The course is Peaked Hill Bar Whistle off the tip of Cape Cod, Jeffrey's Ledge Whistle off the coast of New Hampshire, and return to Manchester.

As the racers may be expected back during the afternoon of the following day, a visit to Manchester, on Sunday Sept. 7, will afford an opportunity of seeing the finish. Tercentenary Jeffrey's Ledge Trophies will be awarded to the first three boats in Class A and in Class B.

September 13

OFF NEWPORT. Commencing Saturday, September 13th, and on each consecutive day except Sunday, races will be held between the *Shamrock*, the challenger, and the yacht selected to defend the *America's* cup until one yacht shall have won four races.

Special trips to the races have been planned by the Eastern Steamship Lines for Sept. 12, 15, 17 and 19. The *S.S. Northland* will sail from Boston on these days at 8.00 P.M. (Standard Time). She will lie in Newport Harbor for the night and on the next day will follow the yachts over the course.

October 6

BOSTON (Charles River Basin). Motor Boat Races held under the auspices of the American Legion National Convention.

It is hoped that among the contenders will be the crews and boats which will race in the national championship the following week at Middletown, Conn.

These races will start at 10.00 A.M. and continue through the day till after 4.00 P.M. There will be five classes racing and two heats in each class.

Tercentenary Trophies will be awarded.

October 8, 9, 10

GLOUCESTER. Fisherman's Races. On these days there will be separate races between fishing schooners which have come in from the Banks. It is expected that the contest will be an international event in which a Nova Scotia fishing schooner will be matched against a Gloucester vessel.

Should the international feature not materialize, then several Gloucester vessels will compete among themselves and satisfy the rivalry which was unsatisfied in the light airs of last season's race.

Purses offered by the Tercentenary Marine Committee will be awarded.